IF FOUND,
PLEASE RETURN TO:

_____

_____

_____

_____

MW00852716

ONE
LINE
A DAY

A FIVE-YEAR
MEMORY BOOK

CHRONICLE BOOKS
SAN FRANCISCO

Kindah Khalidy is an artist based in San Francisco. She is known for exuberant paintings and textile designs that reflect a playful approach to color and form.

ISBN 978-1-4521-7480-8

Manufactured in China.

Artwork by Kindah Khalidy.
Design by Kristen Hewitt.

10 9 8 7 6 5 4 3 2 1

Chronicle Books LLC
680 Second Street
San Francisco, California 94107
www.chroniclebooks.com

A CONDENSED, COMPARATIVE RECORD FOR FIVE YEARS, FOR RECORDING EVENTS MOST WORTHY OF REMEMBRANCE.

HOW TO USE THIS BOOK

To begin, turn to today's calendar date and fill in the year at the top of the page's first entry. Here, you can add your thoughts on the present day's events. On the next day, turn the page and fill in the year accordingly. Do likewise throughout the year. When the year has ended, start the next year in the second entry space on the page, and so on through the remaining years.

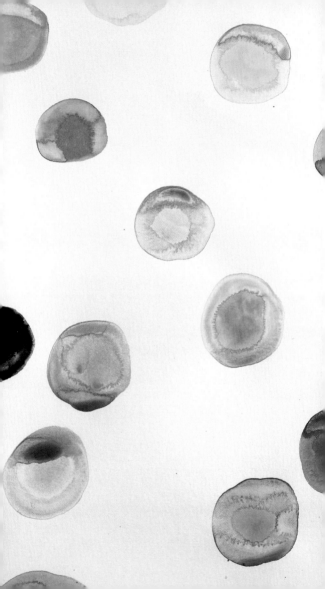

JANUARY 1

20_____ _____

_____

_____

_____

_____

20_____ _____

_____

_____

_____

_____

20_____ _____

_____

_____

_____

_____

20_____ _____

_____

_____

_____

_____

20_____ _____

_____

_____

_____

_____

JANUARY 2

20___ _____

20___ _____

20___ _____

20___ _____

20___ _____

JANUARY 3

20___ _____

_____

_____

_____

_____

20___ _____

_____

_____

_____

_____

20___ _____

_____

_____

_____

_____

20___ _____

_____

_____

_____

_____

20___ _____

_____

_____

_____

JANUARY 4

20___ _____
_____
_____
_____
_____

20___ _____
_____
_____
_____
_____

20___ _____
_____
_____
_____
_____

20___ _____
_____
_____
_____
_____

20___ _____
_____
_____
_____
_____

JANUARY 5

20___ _____
_____
_____
_____
_____

20___ _____
_____
_____
_____
_____

20___ _____
_____
_____
_____
_____

20___ _____
_____
_____
_____
_____

20___ _____
_____
_____
_____
_____

JANUARY 6

20___ _____
_____
_____
_____
_____
_____

20___ _____
_____
_____
_____
_____
_____

20___ _____
_____
_____
_____
_____
_____

20___ _____
_____
_____
_____
_____
_____

20___ _____
_____
_____
_____
_____
_____

JANUARY 7

20___

20___

20___

20___

20___

JANUARY 8

20___ _____

20___ _____

20___ _____

20___ _____

20___ _____

JANUARY 9

20___ _____

20___ _____

20___ _____

20___ _____

20___ _____

JANUARY 10

20____

_____

20____

_____

20____

_____

20____

_____

20____

_____

JANUARY 11

20___ _____

20___ _____

20___ _____

20___ _____

20___ _____

JANUARY 12

20___ _____

20___ _____

20___ _____

20___ _____

20___ _____

JANUARY 13

20___ _____
_____
_____
_____
_____

20___ _____
_____
_____
_____
_____

20___ _____
_____
_____
_____
_____

20___ _____
_____
_____
_____
_____

20___ _____
_____
_____
_____
_____

JANUARY 14

20___ _____

_____

_____

_____

_____

20___ _____

_____

_____

_____

_____

20___ _____

_____

_____

_____

_____

20___ _____

_____

_____

_____

_____

20___ _____

_____

_____

_____

_____

JANUARY 15

20___ _____
_____
_____
_____
_____

20___ _____
_____
_____
_____
_____

20___ _____
_____
_____
_____
_____

20___ _____
_____
_____
_____

20___ _____
_____
_____
_____
_____

JANUARY 16

20____ _____
_____
_____
_____
_____

20____ _____
_____
_____
_____
_____

20____ _____
_____
_____
_____
_____

20____ _____
_____
_____
_____
_____

20____ _____
_____
_____
_____
_____

JANUARY 17

20____ _____

_____

_____

_____

_____

20____ _____

_____

_____

_____

_____

20____ _____

_____

_____

_____

_____

20____ _____

_____

_____

_____

_____

20____ _____

_____

_____

_____

_____

JANUARY 18

20___

20___

20___

20___

20___

JANUARY 19

20___

_____

_____

_____

_____

_____

20___

_____

_____

_____

_____

_____

20___

_____

_____

_____

_____

_____

20___

_____

_____

_____

_____

_____

20___

_____

_____

_____

_____

_____

JANUARY 20

20____ _____

_____

_____

_____

_____

20____ _____

_____

_____

_____

_____

20____ _____

_____

_____

_____

_____

20____ _____

_____

_____

_____

_____

20____ _____

_____

_____

_____

_____

JANUARY 21

20___ _____
_____
_____
_____
_____

20___ _____
_____
_____
_____
_____

20___ _____
_____
_____
_____
_____

20___ _____
_____
_____
_____
_____

20___ _____
_____
_____
_____
_____

JANUARY 22

20____

20____

20____

20____

20____

JANUARY 23

20___ _____
_____
_____
_____
_____

20___ _____
_____
_____
_____
_____

20___ _____
_____
_____
_____
_____

20___ _____
_____
_____
_____
_____

20___ _____
_____
_____
_____
_____

JANUARY 24

20___ _____

20___ _____

20___ _____

20___ _____

20___ _____

JANUARY 25

20___ _____

20___ _____

20___ _____

20___ _____

20___ _____

JANUARY 26

20___ _____

_____

_____

_____

_____

20___ _____

_____

_____

_____

_____

20___ _____

_____

_____

_____

_____

20___ _____

_____

_____

_____

_____

20___ _____

_____

_____

_____

_____

JANUARY 27

20___ _____

_____

_____

_____

_____

20___ _____

_____

_____

_____

_____

20___ _____

_____

_____

_____

_____

20___ _____

_____

_____

_____

_____

20___ _____

_____

_____

_____

JANUARY 28

20___ _____

20___ _____

20___ _____

20___ _____

20___ _____

JANUARY 29

20___ _____

20___ _____

20___ _____

20___ _____

20___ _____

JANUARY 30

20___ _____

20___ _____

20___ _____

20___ _____

20___ _____

JANUARY 31

20___ _____

_____

_____

_____

_____

20___ _____

_____

_____

_____

_____

20___ _____

_____

_____

_____

_____

20___ _____

_____

_____

_____

_____

20___ _____

_____

_____

_____

_____

FEBRUARY 1

20___

_____

_____

_____

_____

20___

_____

_____

_____

_____

20___

_____

_____

_____

_____

20___

_____

_____

_____

_____

20___

_____

_____

_____

_____

FEBRUARY 2

20___

_____

_____

_____

_____

_____

20___

_____

_____

_____

_____

_____

20___

_____

_____

_____

_____

_____

20___

_____

_____

_____

_____

_____

20___

_____

_____

_____

_____

_____

FEBRUARY 3

20____

20____

20____

20____

20____

FEBRUARY 4

20_____ _____

_____

_____

_____

_____

20_____ _____

_____

_____

_____

_____

20_____ _____

_____

_____

_____

20_____ _____

_____

_____

_____

_____

20_____ _____

_____

_____

_____

FEBRUARY 5

20___

20___

20___

20___

20___

FEBRUARY 6

20_____ _____

20_____ _____

20_____ _____

20_____ _____

20_____ _____

FEBRUARY 7

20___

_____
_____
_____
_____
_____

20___

_____
_____
_____
_____
_____

20___

_____
_____
_____
_____

20___

_____
_____
_____
_____

20___

_____
_____
_____
_____

FEBRUARY 8

20___ _____

_____

_____

_____

_____

20___ _____

_____

_____

_____

_____

20___ _____

_____

_____

_____

_____

20___ _____

_____

_____

_____

_____

20___ _____

_____

_____

_____

_____

FEBRUARY 9

20___ _____

_____

_____

_____

_____

20___ _____

_____

_____

_____

_____

20___ _____

_____

_____

_____

_____

20___ _____

_____

_____

_____

_____

20___ _____

_____

_____

_____

_____

FEBRUARY.10

20___ _____

20___ _____

20___ _____

20___ _____

20___ _____

FEBRUARY 11

20___

20___

20___

20___

20___

FEBRUARY 12

20____

_____

_____

_____

_____

_____

20____

_____

_____

_____

_____

_____

20____

_____

_____

_____

_____

_____

20____

_____

_____

_____

_____

_____

20____

_____

_____

_____

_____

FEBRUARY 13

20_____ _____

_____

_____

_____

_____

20_____ _____

_____

_____

_____

_____

20_____ _____

_____

_____

_____

_____

20_____ _____

_____

_____

_____

_____

20_____ _____

_____

_____

_____

_____

FEBRUARY 14

20

_____

20

_____

20

_____

20

_____

20

_____

FEBRUARY 15

20___ _____

_____

_____

_____

_____

_____

20___ _____

_____

_____

_____

_____

_____

20___ _____

_____

_____

_____

_____

20___ _____

_____

_____

_____

_____

20___ _____

_____

_____

_____

_____

FEBRUARY 16

20____

_____

_____

_____

_____

20____

_____

_____

_____

_____

20____

_____

_____

_____

_____

20____

_____

_____

_____

_____

20____

_____

_____

_____

_____

FEBRUARY 17

20___ _____

20___ _____

20___ _____

20___ _____

20___ _____

FEBRUARY. 18

20___ _____

_____

_____

_____

_____

20___ _____

_____

_____

_____

_____

20___ _____

_____

_____

_____

_____

20___ _____

_____

_____

_____

_____

20___ _____

_____

_____

_____

_____

FEBRUARY 19

20

20

20

20

20

FEBRUARY 20●

20___

_____

20___

_____

20___

_____

20___

_____

20___

FEBRUARY 21

20___

20___

20___

20___

20___

FEBRUARY 22

20___ _____

_____

_____

_____

_____

20___ _____

_____

_____

_____

_____

20___ _____

_____

_____

_____

_____

20___ _____

_____

_____

_____

_____

20___ _____

_____

_____

_____

_____

FEBRUARY 23

20___ _____

20___ _____

20___ _____

20___ _____

20___ _____

FEBRUARY 24

20___

20___

20___

20___

20___

FEBRUARY 25

20___ _____

20___ _____

20___ _____

20___ _____

20___ _____

FEBRUARY . 26

20____

_____

_____

_____

_____

_____

20____

_____

_____

_____

_____

_____

20____

_____

_____

_____

_____

_____

20____

_____

_____

_____

_____

_____

20____

_____

_____

_____

_____

_____

FEBRUARY 27

20___

20___

20___

20___

20___

FEBRUARY 28

20___

20___

20___

20___

20___

FEBRUARY 29

20___ _____

20___ _____

20___ _____

20___ _____

20___ _____

MARCH 1

20____ _____

_____

_____

_____

_____

20____ _____

_____

_____

_____

_____

20____ _____

_____

_____

_____

_____

20____ _____

_____

_____

_____

_____

20____ _____

_____

_____

_____

_____

MARCH 2

20___ _____
_____
_____
_____
_____

20___ _____
_____
_____
_____
_____

20___ _____
_____
_____
_____
_____

20___ _____
_____
_____
_____
_____

20___ _____
_____
_____
_____
_____

MARCH 3

20___ _____
_____
_____
_____
_____

20___ _____
_____
_____
_____
_____

20___ _____
_____
_____
_____
_____

20___ _____
_____
_____
_____
_____

20___ _____
_____
_____
_____
_____

MARCH 4

20___ _____
_____
_____
_____
_____

20___ _____
_____
_____
_____
_____

20___ _____
_____
_____
_____
_____

20___ _____
_____
_____
_____
_____

20___ _____
_____
_____
_____
_____

MARCH 5

20_____ _____

20_____ _____

20_____ _____

20_____ _____

20_____ _____

MARCH 6

20___ _____

20___ _____

20___ _____

20___ _____

20___ _____

MARCH 7

20___ _____

_____

_____

_____

_____

20___ _____

_____

_____

_____

_____

20___ _____

_____

_____

_____

_____

20___ _____

_____

_____

_____

_____

20___ _____

_____

_____

_____

_____

MARCH 8

20___ _____
_____
_____
_____
_____

20___ _____
_____
_____
_____
_____

20___ _____
_____
_____
_____
_____

20___ _____
_____
_____
_____
_____

20___ _____
_____
_____
_____
_____

MARCH 9

20____ _____

20____ _____

20____ _____

20____ _____

20____ _____

MARCH 10

20____ _____

_____

_____

_____

_____

20____ _____

_____

_____

_____

_____

20____ _____

_____

_____

_____

_____

20____ _____

_____

_____

_____

_____

20____ _____

_____

_____

_____

_____

MARCH 11

20___ _____
_____
_____
_____
_____

20___ _____
_____
_____
_____
_____

20___ _____
_____
_____
_____
_____

20___ _____
_____
_____
_____
_____

20___ _____
_____
_____
_____
_____

MARCH 12

20___ _____

20___ _____

20___ _____

20___ _____

20___ _____

MARCH 13

20___

_____

_____

_____

_____

_____

20___

_____

_____

_____

_____

_____

20___

_____

_____

_____

_____

_____

20___

_____

_____

_____

_____

_____

20___

_____

_____

_____

_____

_____

MARCH 14

20___ _____

_____

_____

_____

_____

20___ _____

_____

_____

_____

_____

20___ _____

_____

_____

_____

20___ _____

_____

_____

_____

_____

20___ _____

_____

_____

_____

MARCH 15

20___ _____
_____
_____
_____
_____

20___ _____
_____
_____
_____
_____

20___ _____
_____
_____
_____
_____

20___ _____
_____
_____
_____
_____

20___ _____
_____
_____
_____
_____

MARCH 16

20___ _____

20___ _____

20___ _____

20___ _____

20___ _____

MARCH 17

20___ _____
_____
_____
_____
_____

20___ _____
_____
_____
_____
_____

20___ _____
_____
_____
_____
_____

20___ _____
_____
_____
_____
_____

20___ _____
_____
_____
_____
_____

MARCH 18

20___ _____
_____
_____
_____
_____

20___ _____
_____
_____
_____
_____

20___ _____
_____
_____
_____
_____

20___ _____
_____
_____
_____
_____

20___ _____
_____
_____
_____
_____

MARCH 19

20___ _____

20___ _____

20___ _____

20___ _____

20___ _____

MARCH 20

20____

_____

_____

_____

_____

_____

20____

_____

_____

_____

_____

_____

20____

_____

_____

_____

_____

_____

20____

_____

_____

_____

_____

_____

20____

_____

_____

_____

_____

_____

MARCH 21

20___ _____
_____
_____
_____
_____

20___ _____
_____
_____
_____
_____

20___ _____
_____
_____
_____
_____

20___ _____
_____
_____
_____
_____

20___ _____
_____
_____
_____
_____

MARCH 22

20___ _____

20___ _____

20___ _____

20___ _____

20___ _____

MARCH 23

20_____ _____
_____
_____
_____
_____

20_____ _____
_____
_____
_____
_____

20_____ _____
_____
_____
_____
_____

20_____ _____
_____
_____
_____
_____

20_____ _____
_____
_____
_____
_____

MARCH 24

20___ _____

_____

_____

_____

_____

20___ _____

_____

_____

_____

_____

20___ _____

_____

_____

_____

_____

20___ _____

_____

_____

_____

_____

20___ _____

_____

_____

_____

_____

MARCH 25

20___ _____

20___ _____

20___ _____

20___ _____

20___ _____

MARCH 26

20___ _____
_____
_____
_____
_____

20___ _____
_____
_____
_____
_____

20___ _____
_____
_____
_____
_____

20___ _____
_____
_____
_____
_____

20___ _____
_____
_____
_____
_____

MARCH 27

20___ _____
_____
_____
_____
_____

20___ _____
_____
_____
_____
_____

20___ _____
_____
_____
_____
_____

20___ _____
_____
_____
_____

20___ _____
_____
_____
_____
_____

MARCH 28

20___ _____

_____

_____

_____

_____

20___ _____

_____

_____

_____

_____

20___ _____

_____

_____

_____

_____

20___ _____

_____

_____

_____

_____

20___ _____

_____

_____

_____

_____

MARCH 29

20___

20___

20___

20___

20___

MARCH 30

20_____ _____

_____

_____

_____

_____

20_____ _____

_____

_____

_____

_____

20_____ _____

_____

_____

_____

_____

20_____ _____

_____

_____

_____

_____

20_____ _____

_____

_____

_____

_____

MARCH 31

20___ _____
_____
_____
_____
_____

20___ _____
_____
_____
_____
_____

20___ _____
_____
_____
_____
_____

20___ _____
_____
_____
_____
_____

20___ _____
_____
_____
_____
_____

APRIL 1

20____ _____

20____ _____

20____ _____

20____ _____

20____ _____

APRIL 2

20___ _____

20___ _____

20___ _____

20___ _____

20___ _____

APRIL 3

20___

_____

20___

_____

20___

_____

20___

_____

20___

_____

APRIL 4

20___

20___

20___

20___

20___

APRIL 5

20___ _____

20___ _____

20___ _____

20___ _____

20___ _____

APRIL 6

20____

_____

20____

_____

20____

_____

20____

_____

20____

_____

APRIL 7

20___

20___

20___

20___

20___

APRIL 8

20___

20___

20___

20___

20___

APRIL 9

20____

20____

20____

20____

20____

APRIL 10

20___ _____

_____

_____

_____

_____

20___ _____

_____

_____

_____

_____

20___ _____

_____

_____

_____

_____

20___ _____

_____

_____

_____

_____

20___ _____

_____

_____

_____

_____

APRIL 11

20___ _____

20___ _____

20___ _____

20___ _____

20___ _____

APRIL 12

20____ _____

20____ _____

20____ _____

20____ _____

20____ _____

APRIL 13

20___ _____

20___ _____

20___ _____

20___ _____

20___ _____

APRIL 14

20___

20___

20___

20___

20___

APRIL 15

20___

20___

20___

20___

20___

APRIL 16

20___

20___

20___

20___

20___

APRIL 17

20____ _____

20____ _____

20____ _____

20____ _____

20____ _____

APRIL 18

20___ _____

20___ _____

20___ _____

20___ _____

20___ _____

APRIL 19

20___ _____

20___ _____

20___ _____

20___ _____

20___ _____

APRIL 20

20___

20___

20___

20___

20___

APRIL 21

20___

20___

20___

20___

20___

APRIL 22

20___ _____

20___ _____

20___ _____

20___ _____

20___ _____

APRIL 23

20___

20___

20___

20___

20___

APRIL 24

20___

20___

20___

20___

20___

APRIL 25

20___

20___

20___

20___

20___

APRIL 26

20___ _____

20___ _____

20___ _____

20___ _____

20___ _____

APRIL 27

20___ _____

_____

_____

_____

_____

20___ _____

_____

_____

_____

_____

20___ _____

_____

_____

_____

_____

20___ _____

_____

_____

_____

_____

20___ _____

_____

_____

_____

_____

APRIL 28

20___ _____
_____
_____
_____
_____

20___ _____
_____
_____
_____
_____

20___ _____
_____
_____
_____
_____

20___ _____
_____
_____
_____
_____

20___ _____
_____
_____
_____
_____

APRIL 29

20___

20___

20___

20___

20___

APRIL 30

20___

20___

20___

20___

20___

MAY 1

20___ _____

_____

_____

_____

_____

20___ _____

_____

_____

_____

_____

20___ _____

_____

_____

_____

_____

20___ _____

_____

_____

_____

_____

20___ _____

_____

_____

_____

_____

MAY 2

20___

20___

20___

20___

20___

MAY 3

20___ _____
_____
_____
_____
_____

20___ _____
_____
_____
_____
_____

20___ _____
_____
_____
_____
_____

20___ _____
_____
_____
_____
_____

20___ _____
_____
_____
_____
_____

MAY 4

20___ _____

_____

_____

_____

_____

20___ _____

_____

_____

_____

_____

20___ _____

_____

_____

_____

_____

20___ _____

_____

_____

_____

_____

20___ _____

_____

_____

_____

_____

MAY 5

20___

20___

20___

20___

20___

MAY 6

20___ _____
_____
_____
_____
_____
_____

20___ _____
_____
_____
_____
_____
_____

20___ _____
_____
_____
_____
_____
_____

20___ _____
_____
_____
_____
_____
_____

20___ _____
_____
_____
_____
_____
_____

MAY 7

20___

_____

_____

_____

_____

_____

20___

_____

_____

_____

_____

_____

20___

_____

_____

_____

_____

_____

20___

_____

_____

_____

_____

_____

20___

_____

_____

_____

_____

_____

MAY 8

20___ _____

_____

_____

_____

_____

_____

20___ _____

_____

_____

_____

_____

_____

20___ _____

_____

_____

_____

_____

_____

20___ _____

_____

_____

_____

_____

20___ _____

_____

_____

_____

_____

MAY 9

20___

_____

_____

_____

_____

_____

20___

_____

_____

_____

_____

_____

20___

_____

_____

_____

_____

_____

20___

_____

_____

_____

_____

_____

20___

_____

_____

_____

_____

MAY 10

20___ _____

_____

_____

_____

_____

20___ _____

_____

_____

_____

_____

20___ _____

_____

_____

_____

_____

20___ _____

_____

_____

_____

_____

20___ _____

_____

_____

_____

_____

MAY 11

20____ _____

_____

_____

_____

_____

20____ _____

_____

_____

_____

_____

20____ _____

_____

_____

_____

_____

20____ _____

_____

_____

_____

_____

20____ _____

_____

_____

_____

_____

MAY 12

20___ _____

_____
_____
_____
_____
_____

20___ _____

_____
_____
_____
_____
_____

20___ _____

_____
_____
_____
_____
_____

20___ _____

_____
_____
_____
_____
_____

20___ _____

_____
_____
_____
_____

MAY 13

20 _____

20 _____

20 _____

20 _____

20 _____

MAY 14

20___

_____

_____

_____

_____

_____

20___

_____

_____

_____

_____

_____

20___

_____

_____

_____

_____

_____

20___

_____

_____

_____

_____

_____

20___

_____

_____

_____

_____

_____

MAY 15

20___ _____
_____
_____
_____
_____

20___ _____
_____
_____
_____
_____

20___ _____
_____
_____
_____
_____

20___ _____
_____
_____
_____
_____

20___ _____
_____
_____
_____
_____

MAY 16

20___ _____

_____

_____

_____

_____

20___ _____

_____

_____

_____

_____

20___ _____

_____

_____

_____

_____

20___ _____

_____

_____

_____

_____

20___ _____

_____

_____

_____

_____

MAY 17

20___ _____

_____

_____

_____

_____

20___ _____

_____

_____

_____

_____

20___ _____

_____

_____

_____

_____

20___ _____

_____

_____

_____

_____

20___ _____

_____

_____

_____

_____

MAY 18

20____

_____

_____

_____

_____

_____

20____

_____

_____

_____

_____

_____

20____

_____

_____

_____

_____

_____

20____

_____

_____

_____

_____

_____

20____

_____

_____

_____

_____

_____

MAY 19

20___ _____
_____
_____
_____
_____
_____

20___ _____
_____
_____
_____
_____
_____

20___ _____
_____
_____
_____
_____
_____

20___ _____
_____
_____
_____
_____
_____

20___ _____
_____
_____
_____
_____

MAY 20

20_____ _____

_____
_____
_____
_____

20_____ _____

_____
_____
_____
_____

20_____ _____

_____
_____
_____
_____

20_____ _____

_____
_____
_____
_____

20_____ _____

_____
_____
_____
_____

MAY 21

20___

_____

_____

_____

_____

_____

20___

_____

_____

_____

_____

_____

20___

_____

_____

_____

_____

_____

20___

_____

_____

_____

_____

_____

20___

_____

_____

_____

_____

_____

MAY 22

20_____ _____

_____
_____
_____
_____

20_____ _____

_____
_____
_____
_____

20_____ _____

_____
_____
_____
_____

20_____ _____

_____
_____
_____
_____

20_____ _____

_____
_____
_____
_____

MAY 23

20___ _____
_____
_____
_____
_____

20___ _____
_____
_____
_____
_____

20___ _____
_____
_____
_____
_____

20___ _____
_____
_____
_____
_____

20___ _____
_____
_____
_____
_____

MAY 24

20___ _____
_____
_____
_____
_____
_____

20___ _____
_____
_____
_____
_____
_____

20___ _____
_____
_____
_____
_____
_____

20___ _____
_____
_____
_____
_____
_____

20___ _____
_____
_____
_____
_____
_____

MAY 25

20___ _____

_____

_____

_____

_____

20___ _____

_____

_____

_____

_____

20___ _____

_____

_____

_____

_____

20___ _____

_____

_____

_____

_____

20___ _____

_____

_____

_____

_____

MAY 26

20____ _____

_____

_____

_____

_____

20____ _____

_____

_____

_____

_____

20____ _____

_____

_____

_____

_____

20____ _____

_____

_____

_____

_____

20____ _____

_____

_____

_____

_____

MAY 27

20___ _____

20___ _____

20___ _____

20___ _____

20___ _____

MAY 28

20___ _____

20___ _____

20___ _____

20___ _____

20___ _____

MAY 29

20___ _____
_____
_____
_____
_____
_____

20___ _____
_____
_____
_____
_____
_____

20___ _____
_____
_____
_____
_____
_____

20___ _____
_____
_____
_____
_____
_____

20___ _____
_____
_____
_____
_____

MAY 30

20___ _____

_____

_____

_____

_____

_____

20___ _____

_____

_____

_____

_____

_____

20___ _____

_____

_____

_____

_____

_____

20___ _____

_____

_____

_____

_____

_____

20___ _____

_____

_____

_____

_____

MAY 31

20___ _____

_____

_____

_____

_____

20___ _____

_____

_____

_____

_____

20___ _____

_____

_____

_____

_____

20___ _____

_____

_____

_____

_____

20___ _____

_____

_____

_____

_____

JUNE 1

20___ _____

20___ _____

20___ _____

20___ _____

20___ _____

JUNE 2

20___ _____
_____
_____
_____
_____

20___ _____
_____
_____
_____
_____

20___ _____
_____
_____
_____
_____

20___ _____
_____
_____
_____
_____

20___ _____
_____
_____
_____
_____

JUNE 3

20___

20___

20___

20___

20___

JUNE 4

20___ _____
_____
_____
_____
_____

20___ _____
_____
_____
_____
_____

20___ _____
_____
_____
_____
_____

20___ _____
_____
_____
_____
_____

20___ _____
_____
_____
_____
_____

JUNE 5

20___ _____
_____
_____
_____
_____
_____

20___ _____
_____
_____
_____
_____
_____

20___ _____
_____
_____
_____
_____
_____

20___ _____
_____
_____
_____
_____
_____

20___ _____
_____
_____
_____
_____

JUNE 6

20___ _____
_____
_____
_____
_____

20___ _____
_____
_____
_____
_____

20___ _____
_____
_____
_____

20___ _____
_____
_____
_____
_____

20___ _____
_____
_____
_____
_____

JUNE 7

20___ _____

20___ _____

20___ _____

20___ _____

20___ _____

JUNE 8

20___ _____

20___ _____

20___ _____

20___ _____

20___ _____

JUNE 9

20___ _____
_____
_____
_____
_____

20___ _____
_____
_____
_____
_____

20___ _____
_____
_____
_____
_____

20___ _____
_____
_____
_____
_____

20___ _____
_____
_____
_____
_____

JUNE 10

20_____

20_____

20_____

20_____

20_____

JUNE 11

20___ _____
_____
_____
_____
_____

20___ _____
_____
_____
_____
_____

20___ _____
_____
_____
_____
_____

20___ _____
_____
_____
_____
_____

20___ _____
_____
_____
_____

JUNE 12

20___

20___

20___

20___

20___

JUNE 13

20____ _____
_____
_____
_____
_____

20____ _____
_____
_____
_____
_____

20____ _____
_____
_____
_____
_____

20____ _____
_____
_____
_____
_____

20____ _____
_____
_____
_____
_____

JUNE 14

20___ _____
_____
_____
_____
_____

20___ _____
_____
_____
_____
_____

20___ _____
_____
_____
_____
_____

20___ _____
_____
_____
_____
_____

20___ _____
_____
_____
_____
_____

JUNE 15

20___ _____

20___ _____

20___ _____

20___ _____

20___ _____

JUNE 16

20___ _____
_____
_____
_____
_____

20___ _____
_____
_____
_____
_____
_____

20___ _____
_____
_____
_____
_____

20___ _____
_____
_____
_____

20___ _____
_____
_____
_____

JUNE 17

20___

20___

20___

20___

20___

JUNE 18

20___ _____

20___ _____

20___ _____

20___ _____

20___ _____

JUNE 19

20___ _____
_____
_____
_____
_____

20___ _____
_____
_____
_____
_____

20___ _____
_____
_____
_____
_____

20___ _____
_____
_____
_____
_____

20___ _____
_____
_____
_____
_____

JUNE 20

20____ _____
_____
_____
_____
_____

20____ _____
_____
_____
_____
_____

20____ _____
_____
_____
_____
_____

20____ _____
_____
_____
_____
_____

20____ _____
_____
_____
_____
_____

JUNE 21

20___ _____

_____

_____

_____

_____

20___ _____

_____

_____

_____

_____

20___ _____

_____

_____

_____

_____

20___ _____

_____

_____

_____

_____

20___ _____

_____

_____

_____

_____

JUNE 22

20___ _____
_____
_____
_____
_____

20___ _____
_____
_____
_____
_____

20___ _____
_____
_____
_____
_____

20___ _____
_____
_____
_____
_____

20___ _____
_____
_____
_____
_____

JUNE 23

20___ _____
_____
_____
_____
_____

20___ _____
_____
_____
_____
_____

20___ _____
_____
_____
_____
_____

20___ _____
_____
_____
_____

20___ _____
_____
_____
_____

JUNE 24

20___ _____
_____
_____
_____
_____

20___ _____
_____
_____
_____
_____

20___ _____
_____
_____
_____
_____

20___ _____
_____
_____
_____
_____

20___ _____
_____
_____
_____
_____

JUNE 25

20___ _____

20___ _____

20___ _____

20___ _____

20___ _____

JUNE 26

20___ _____

_____

_____

_____

_____

20___ _____

_____

_____

_____

_____

20___ _____

_____

_____

_____

_____

20___ _____

_____

_____

_____

_____

20___ _____

_____

_____

_____

JUNE 27

20___ _____

20___ _____

20___ _____

20___ _____

20___ _____

JUNE 28

20___ _____

20___ _____

20___ _____

20___ _____

20___ _____

JUNE 29

20___

20___

20___

20___

20___

JUNE 30

20___ _____
_____
_____
_____
_____

20___ _____
_____
_____
_____
_____

20___ _____
_____
_____
_____
_____

20___ _____
_____
_____
_____
_____

20___ _____
_____
_____
_____
_____

JULY 1

20___ _____
_____
_____
_____
_____

20___ _____
_____
_____
_____
_____

20___ _____
_____
_____
_____
_____

20___ _____
_____
_____
_____
_____

20___ _____
_____
_____
_____
_____

JULY 2

20___ _____

20___ _____

20___ _____

20___ _____

20___ _____

JULY 3

20___ _____
_____
_____
_____
_____

20___ _____
_____
_____
_____
_____

20___ _____
_____
_____
_____
_____

20___ _____
_____
_____
_____
_____

20___ _____
_____
_____
_____
_____

JULY 4

20___

20___

20___

20___

20___

JULY 5

20____

_____

_____

_____

_____

_____

20____

_____

_____

_____

_____

_____

20____

_____

_____

_____

_____

_____

20____

_____

_____

_____

_____

_____

20____

_____

_____

_____

_____

_____

JULY 6

20___ _____

20___ _____

20___ _____

20___ _____

20___ _____

JULY 7

20___ _____

20___ _____

20___ _____

20___ _____

20___ _____

JULY 8

20___ _____

20___ _____

20___ _____

20___ _____

20___ _____

JULY 9

20___ _____

20___ _____

20___ _____

20___ _____

20___ _____

JULY 10

20___ _____

20___ _____

20___ _____

20___ _____

20___ _____

JULY 11.

20___ _____

20___ _____

20___ _____

20___ _____

20___ _____

JULY 12

20___

20___

20___

20___

20___

JULY 13

20___ _____
_____
_____
_____
_____

20___ _____
_____
_____
_____
_____

20___ _____
_____
_____
_____
_____

20___ _____
_____
_____
_____
_____

20___ _____
_____
_____
_____
_____

JULY 14

20____ _____

20____ _____

20____ _____

20____ _____

20____ _____

JULY 15

20___ _____

_____

_____

_____

_____

20___ _____

_____

_____

_____

_____

20___ _____

_____

_____

_____

_____

20___ _____

_____

_____

_____

_____

20___ _____

_____

_____

_____

_____

JULY 16

20___ _____
_____
_____
_____
_____

20___ _____
_____
_____
_____
_____

20___ _____
_____
_____
_____
_____

20___ _____
_____
_____
_____
_____

20___ _____
_____
_____
_____
_____

JULY 17

20___ _____

20___ _____

20___ _____

20___ _____

20___ _____

JULY 18

20___ _____

20___ _____

20___ _____

20___ _____

20___ _____

JULY 19

20___ _____

20___ _____

20___ _____

20___ _____

20___ _____

JULY 20

20___

20___

20___

20___

20___

JULY 21

20___ _____
_____
_____
_____
_____

20___ _____
_____
_____
_____
_____

20___ _____
_____
_____
_____
_____

20___ _____
_____
_____
_____
_____

20___ _____
_____
_____
_____
_____

JULY 22

20___ _____

_____

_____

_____

_____

20___ _____

_____

_____

_____

_____

20___ _____

_____

_____

_____

_____

20___ _____

_____

_____

_____

_____

20___ _____

_____

_____

_____

_____

JULY 23

20___ _____

20___ _____

20___ _____

20___ _____

20___ _____

JULY 24

20___ _____

_____

_____

_____

_____

20___ _____

_____

_____

_____

_____

20___ _____

_____

_____

_____

_____

20___ _____

_____

_____

_____

_____

20___ _____

_____

_____

_____

_____

JULY 25

20___ _____

20___ _____

20___ _____

20___ _____

20___ _____

JULY 26

20___ _____

20___ _____

20___ _____

20___ _____

20___ _____

JULY 27

20___ _____

20___ _____

20___ _____

20___ _____

20___ _____

JULY 28

20___

20___

20___

20___

20___

JULY 29

20___ _____

_____

_____

_____

_____

20___ _____

_____

_____

_____

_____

20___ _____

_____

_____

_____

_____

20___ _____

_____

_____

_____

_____

20___ _____

_____

_____

_____

_____

JULY 30

20___ _____
_____
_____
_____

20___ _____
_____
_____
_____

20___ _____
_____
_____
_____

20___ _____
_____
_____
_____

20___ _____
_____
_____
_____

JULY 31

20___ _____

20___ _____

20___ _____

20___ _____

20___ _____

AUGUST 1

20___ _____
_____
_____
_____
_____

20___ _____
_____
_____
_____
_____

20___ _____
_____
_____
_____
_____

20___ _____
_____
_____
_____
_____

20___ _____
_____
_____
_____
_____

AUGUST 2

20___ _____

_____

_____

_____

_____

20___ _____

_____

_____

_____

_____

20___ _____

_____

_____

_____

_____

20___ _____

_____

_____

_____

_____

20___ _____

_____

_____

_____

_____

AUGUST 3

20___ _____

20___ _____

20___ _____

20___ _____

20___ _____

AUGUST 4

20___

20___

20___

20___

20___

AUGUST 5

20___ _____

20___ _____

20___ _____

20___ _____

20___ _____

AUGUST 6

20_____ _____

_____

_____

_____

_____

20_____ _____

_____

_____

_____

_____

20_____ _____

_____

_____

_____

_____

20_____ _____

_____

_____

_____

_____

20_____ _____

_____

_____

_____

AUGUST 7

20___ _____
_____
_____
_____
_____

20___ _____
_____
_____
_____
_____

20___ _____
_____
_____
_____
_____

20___ _____
_____
_____
_____
_____

20___ _____
_____
_____
_____
_____

AUGUST 8

20___ _____
_____
_____
_____
_____

20___ _____
_____
_____
_____
_____

20___ _____
_____
_____
_____
_____

20___ _____
_____
_____
_____
_____

20___ _____
_____
_____
_____
_____

AUGUST 9

20___ _____
_____
_____
_____
_____

20___ _____
_____
_____
_____
_____

20___ _____
_____
_____
_____
_____

20___ _____
_____
_____
_____
_____

20___ _____
_____
_____
_____
_____

AUGUST 10

20___ _____

_____

_____

_____

_____

20___ _____

_____

_____

_____

_____

20___ _____

_____

_____

_____

_____

20___ _____

_____

_____

_____

20___ _____

_____

_____

_____

_____

AUGUST 11

20___ _____

_____

_____

_____

_____

20___ _____

_____

_____

_____

_____

20___ _____

_____

_____

_____

_____

20___ _____

_____

_____

_____

_____

20___ _____

_____

_____

_____

AUGUST 12

20___ _____

_____

_____

_____

_____

20___ _____

_____

_____

_____

_____

20___ _____

_____

_____

_____

_____

20___ _____

_____

_____

_____

_____

20___ _____

_____

_____

_____

_____

AUGUST 13

20___

20___

20___

20___

20___

AUGUST 14

20___ _____

_____

_____

_____

_____

20___ _____

_____

_____

_____

_____

20___ _____

_____

_____

_____

_____

20___ _____

_____

_____

_____

_____

20___ _____

_____

_____

_____

_____

AUGUST 15

20___ _____

_____

_____

_____

_____

_____

20___ _____

_____

_____

_____

_____

_____

20___ _____

_____

_____

_____

_____

_____

20___ _____

_____

_____

_____

_____

_____

20___ _____

_____

_____

_____

_____

AUGUST 16

20___

_____

_____

_____

_____

_____

20___

_____

_____

_____

_____

_____

20___

_____

_____

_____

_____

_____

20___

_____

_____

_____

_____

_____

20___

_____

_____

_____

_____

AUGUST 17

20___

20___

20___

20___

20___

AUGUST 18

20___ _____

_____

_____

_____

_____

20___ _____

_____

_____

_____

_____

20___ _____

_____

_____

_____

_____

20___ _____

_____

_____

_____

_____

20___ _____

_____

_____

_____

_____

AUGUST 19

20___ _____

_____

_____

_____

20___ _____

_____

_____

_____

20___ _____

_____

_____

_____

20___ _____

_____

_____

_____

20___ _____

_____

_____

_____

AUGUST 20

20___ _____

_____

_____

_____

_____

20___ _____

_____

_____

_____

_____

20___ _____

_____

_____

_____

_____

20___ _____

_____

_____

_____

_____

20___ _____

_____

_____

_____

_____

AUGUST 21

20___ _____

_____

_____

_____

_____

20___ _____

_____

_____

_____

_____

20___ _____

_____

_____

_____

_____

20___ _____

_____

_____

_____

_____

20___ _____

_____

_____

_____

_____

AUGUST 22

20___ _____

_____

_____

_____

_____

20___ _____

_____

_____

_____

_____

20___ _____

_____

_____

_____

_____

20___ _____

_____

_____

_____

_____

20___ _____

_____

_____

_____

_____

AUGUST 23

20___

_____

_____

_____

_____

_____

20___

_____

_____

_____

_____

_____

20___

_____

_____

_____

_____

_____

20___

_____

_____

_____

_____

_____

20___

_____

_____

_____

_____

_____

AUGUST 24

20___ _____

20___ _____

20___ _____

20___ _____

20___ _____

AUGUST 25

20___ _____
_____
_____
_____
_____

20___ _____
_____
_____
_____
_____

20___ _____
_____
_____
_____
_____

20___ _____
_____
_____
_____
_____

20___ _____
_____
_____
_____
_____

AUGUST 26

20___ _____

_____

_____

_____

_____

20___ _____

_____

_____

_____

_____

20___ _____

_____

_____

_____

_____

20___ _____

_____

_____

_____

20___ _____

_____

_____

_____

_____

AUGUST 27

20____ _____

20____ _____

20____ _____

20____ _____

20____ _____

AUGUST 28

20___ _____
_____
_____
_____
_____

20___ _____
_____
_____
_____
_____

20___ _____
_____
_____
_____
_____

20___ _____
_____
_____
_____
_____

20___ _____
_____
_____
_____
_____

AUGUST 29

20___ _____

20___ _____

20___ _____

20___ _____

20___ _____

AUGUST 30

20___

20___

20___

20___

20___

AUGUST 31

20____ _____

_____

_____

_____

_____

20____ _____

_____

_____

_____

_____

20____ _____

_____

_____

_____

_____

20____ _____

_____

_____

_____

_____

20____ _____

_____

_____

_____

_____

SEPTEMBER 1

20_____ _____

20_____ _____

20_____ _____

20_____ _____

20_____ _____

SEPTEMBER 2

20___ _____

_____

_____

_____

_____

20___ _____

_____

_____

_____

_____

20___ _____

_____

_____

_____

_____

20___ _____

_____

_____

_____

_____

20___ _____

_____

_____

_____

_____

SEPTEMBER 3

20___ _____

20___ _____

20___ _____

20___ _____

20___ _____

SEPTEMBER 4

20___

_____

_____

_____

_____

_____

20___

_____

_____

_____

_____

_____

20___

_____

_____

_____

_____

_____

20___

_____

_____

_____

_____

_____

20___

_____

_____

_____

_____

_____

SEPTEMBER 5

20_____

_____

_____

_____

_____

_____

20_____

_____

_____

_____

_____

_____

20_____

_____

_____

_____

_____

_____

20_____

_____

_____

_____

_____

_____

20_____

_____

_____

_____

_____

_____

SEPTEMBER 6

20___

20___

20___

20___

20___

SEPTEMBER 7

20___

_____

_____

_____

_____

20___

_____

_____

_____

_____

20___

_____

_____

_____

_____

20___

_____

_____

_____

_____

20___

_____

_____

_____

_____

SEPTEMBER 8

20___ _____

20___ _____

20___ _____

20___ _____

20___ _____

SEPTEMBER 9

20____

_____

_____

_____

_____

_____

_____

20____

_____

_____

_____

_____

_____

_____

20____

_____

_____

_____

_____

_____

20____

_____

_____

_____

_____

_____

20____

_____

_____

_____

_____

_____

SEPTEMBER 10

20___

20___

20___

20___

20___

SEPTEMBER 11

20___

_____

20___

_____

20___

_____

20___

_____

20___

_____

SEPTEMBER 12

20___

20___

20___

20___

20___

SEPTEMBER. 13

20____

_____

_____

_____

_____

20____

_____

_____

_____

_____

20____

_____

_____

_____

_____

20____

_____

_____

_____

_____

20____

_____

_____

_____

_____

SEPTEMBER 14

20___

20___

20___

20___

20___

SEPTEMBER 15

20_____ _____

_____

_____

_____

_____

20_____ _____

_____

_____

_____

_____

20_____ _____

_____

_____

_____

_____

20_____ _____

_____

_____

_____

_____

20_____ _____

_____

_____

_____

_____

SEPTEMBER 16

20 _____

_____

_____

_____

_____

20 _____

_____

_____

_____

_____

20 _____

_____

_____

_____

_____

20 _____

_____

_____

_____

_____

20 _____

_____

_____

_____

_____

SEPTEMBER 17

20___

20___

20___

20___

20___

SEPTEMBER 18

20___

_____

20___

_____

20___

_____

20___

_____

20___

_____

SEPTEMBER 19

20___ _____

20___ _____

20___ _____

20___ _____

20___ _____

SEPTEMBER 20

20___

20___

20___

20___

20___

SEPTEMBER. 21

20___ _____

20___ _____

20___ _____

20___ _____

20___ _____

SEPTEMBER 22

20___

20___

20___

20___

20___

SEPTEMBER 23

20___ _____

_____

_____

_____

_____

20___ _____

_____

_____

_____

_____

20___ _____

_____

_____

_____

_____

20___ _____

_____

_____

_____

_____

20___ _____

_____

_____

_____

_____

SEPTEMBER 24

20____ _____

_____

_____

_____

_____

20____ _____

_____

_____

_____

_____

20____ _____

_____

_____

_____

20____ _____

_____

_____

_____

20____ _____

_____

_____

_____

SEPTEMBER 25

20____ _____

_____

_____

_____

_____

20____ _____

_____

_____

_____

_____

20____ _____

_____

_____

_____

_____

20____ _____

_____

_____

_____

_____

20____ _____

_____

_____

_____

SEPTEMBER 26

20___

20___

20___

20___

20___

SEPTEMBER 27

20____

_____

_____

_____

_____

20____

_____

_____

_____

_____

20____

_____

_____

_____

_____

20____

_____

_____

_____

_____

20____

_____

_____

_____

_____

SEPTEMBER 28

20___ _____
_____
_____
_____
_____

20___ _____
_____
_____
_____
_____

20___ _____
_____
_____
_____
_____

20___ _____
_____
_____
_____
_____

20___ _____
_____
_____
_____

SEPTEMBER. 29

20___

20___

20___

20___

20___

SEPTEMBER 30

20___

20___

20___

20___

20___

OCTOBER 1

20___ _____

_____

_____

_____

_____

20___ _____

_____

_____

_____

_____

20___ _____

_____

_____

_____

_____

20___ _____

_____

_____

_____

_____

20___ _____

_____

_____

_____

OCTOBER 2

20 _____ _____

_____

_____

_____

20 _____ _____

_____

_____

_____

20 _____ _____

_____

_____

_____

20 _____ _____

_____

_____

_____

20 _____ _____

_____

_____

_____

OCTOBER 3

20___

20___

20___

20___

20___

OCTOBER 4

20___ _____

_____

_____

_____

20___ _____

_____

_____

_____

20___ _____

_____

_____

_____

20___ _____

_____

_____

_____

20___ _____

_____

_____

_____

OCTOBER 5

20___ _____

_____

_____

_____

_____

20___ _____

_____

_____

_____

_____

20___ _____

_____

_____

_____

_____

20___ _____

_____

_____

_____

_____

20___ _____

_____

_____

_____

_____

OCTOBER 6

20___

20___

20___

20___

20___

OCTOBER 7

20____

_____

20____

_____

20____

_____

20____

_____

20____

_____

OCTOBER 8

20___

20___

20___

20___

20___

OCTOBER 9

20___ _____

_____

_____

_____

_____

20___ _____

_____

_____

_____

_____

20___ _____

_____

_____

_____

_____

20___ _____

_____

_____

_____

_____

20___ _____

_____

_____

_____

_____

OCTOBER 10

20___ _____

_____

_____

_____

_____

20___ _____

_____

_____

_____

_____

20___ _____

_____

_____

_____

_____

20___ _____

_____

_____

_____

_____

20___ _____

_____

_____

_____

_____

OCTOBER 11

20___ _____

_____

_____

_____

_____

20___ _____

_____

_____

_____

_____

20___ _____

_____

_____

_____

_____

20___ _____

_____

_____

_____

_____

20___ _____

_____

_____

_____

_____

OCTOBER 12

20___ _____

_____

_____

_____

_____

20___ _____

_____

_____

_____

_____

20___ _____

_____

_____

_____

_____

20___ _____

_____

_____

_____

_____

20___ _____

_____

_____

_____

_____

OCTOBER 13

20___ _____

20___ _____

20___ _____

20___ _____

20___ _____

OCTOBER 14

20___ _____

20___ _____

20___ _____

20___ _____

20___ _____

OCTOBER 15

20___ _____
_____
_____
_____
_____

20___ _____
_____
_____
_____
_____

20___ _____
_____
_____
_____
_____

20___ _____
_____
_____
_____
_____

20___ _____
_____
_____
_____
_____

OCTOBER 16

20_____

_____

_____

_____

_____

20_____

_____

_____

_____

_____

20_____

_____

_____

_____

_____

20_____

_____

_____

_____

_____

20_____

_____

_____

_____

_____

OCTOBER 17

20___ _____

_____

_____

_____

_____

20___ _____

_____

_____

_____

_____

20___ _____

_____

_____

_____

_____

20___ _____

_____

_____

_____

_____

20___ _____

_____

_____

_____

_____

OCTOBER 18

20___ _____

20___ _____

20___ _____

20___ _____

20___ _____

OCTOBER 19

20____

20____

20____

20____

20____

OCTOBER 20

20___ _____

20___ _____

20___ _____

20___ _____

20___ _____

OCTOBER 21

20___

_____

_____

_____

_____

_____

20___

_____

_____

_____

_____

_____

20___

_____

_____

_____

_____

20___

_____

_____

_____

_____

20___

_____

_____

_____

_____

OCTOBER 22

20___ _____
_____
_____
_____
_____

20___ _____
_____
_____
_____
_____

20___ _____
_____
_____
_____
_____

20___ _____
_____
_____
_____
_____

20___ _____
_____
_____
_____
_____

OCTOBER 23

20___ _____

_____

_____

_____

_____

20___ _____

_____

_____

_____

_____

20___ _____

_____

_____

_____

_____

20___ _____

_____

_____

_____

_____

20___ _____

_____

_____

_____

_____

OCTOBER 24

20___

20___

20___

20___

20___

OCTOBER 25

20___ _____
_____
_____
_____
_____

20___ _____
_____
_____
_____
_____

20___ _____
_____
_____
_____
_____

20___ _____
_____
_____
_____
_____

20___ _____
_____
_____
_____

OCTOBER 26

20___ _____

_____

_____

_____

_____

20___ _____

_____

_____

_____

_____

20___ _____

_____

_____

_____

_____

20___ _____

_____

_____

_____

_____

20___ _____

_____

_____

_____

_____

OCTOBER 27

20___ _____

20___ _____

20___ _____

20___ _____

20___ _____

OCTOBER 28

20___ _____

_____

_____

_____

_____

20___ _____

_____

_____

_____

_____

20___ _____

_____

_____

_____

_____

20___ _____

_____

_____

_____

_____

20___ _____

_____

_____

_____

_____

OCTOBER 29

20___

20___

20___

20___

20___

OCTOBER 30

20___ _____

20___ _____

20___ _____

20___ _____

20___ _____

OCTOBER 31

20___ _____

_____

_____

_____

_____

20___ _____

_____

_____

_____

_____

20___ _____

_____

_____

_____

_____

20___ _____

_____

_____

_____

_____

20___ _____

_____

_____

_____

_____

NOVEMBER 1

20___

_____

_____

_____

_____

_____

20___

_____

_____

_____

_____

_____

20___

_____

_____

_____

_____

_____

20___

_____

_____

_____

_____

_____

20___

_____

_____

_____

_____

_____

NOVEMBER 2

20___ _____

_____

_____

_____

_____

20___ _____

_____

_____

_____

_____

_____

20___ _____

_____

_____

_____

_____

20___ _____

_____

_____

_____

_____

20___ _____

_____

_____

_____

NOVEMBER 3

20___ _____

20___ _____

20___ _____

20___ _____

20___ _____

NOVEMBER 4

20____ _____

20____ _____

20____ _____

20____ _____

20____ _____

NOVEMBER 5

20___ _____

20___ _____

20___ _____

20___ _____

20___ _____

NOVEMBER 6

20____ _____

_____

_____

_____

_____

20____ _____

_____

_____

_____

_____

20____ _____

_____

_____

_____

_____

20____ _____

_____

_____

_____

_____

20____ _____

_____

_____

_____

_____

NOVEMBER 7

20___ _____

_____

_____

_____

_____

20___ _____

_____

_____

_____

_____

20___ _____

_____

_____

_____

_____

20___ _____

_____

_____

_____

_____

20___ _____

_____

_____

_____

NOVEMBER 8

20___ _____
_____
_____
_____
_____

20___ _____
_____
_____
_____
_____

20___ _____
_____
_____
_____
_____

20___ _____
_____
_____
_____
_____

20___ _____
_____
_____
_____
_____

NOVEMBER 9

20____

20____

20____

20____

20____

NOVEMBER 10

20___ _____

_____

_____

_____

_____

20___ _____

_____

_____

_____

_____

20___ _____

_____

_____

_____

_____

20___ _____

_____

_____

_____

_____

20___ _____

_____

_____

_____

_____

NOVEMBER 11

20___

_____

_____

_____

_____

_____

20___

_____

_____

_____

_____

_____

20___

_____

_____

_____

_____

_____

20___

_____

_____

_____

_____

_____

20___

_____

_____

_____

_____

_____

NOVEMBER 12

20___ _____

_____

_____

_____

_____

20___ _____

_____

_____

_____

_____

20___ _____

_____

_____

_____

_____

20___ _____

_____

_____

_____

_____

20___ _____

_____

_____

_____

_____

NOVEMBER 13

20___ _____
_____
_____
_____
_____

20___ _____
_____
_____
_____
_____

20___ _____
_____
_____
_____
_____

20___ _____
_____
_____
_____
_____

20___ _____
_____
_____
_____
_____

NOVEMBER 14

20___ _____
_____
_____
_____
_____

20___ _____
_____
_____
_____
_____

20___ _____
_____
_____
_____
_____

20___ _____
_____
_____
_____
_____

20___ _____
_____
_____
_____
_____

NOVEMBER 15

20___

_____

_____

_____

_____

_____

20___

_____

_____

_____

_____

_____

20___

_____

_____

_____

_____

_____

20___

_____

_____

_____

_____

_____

20___

_____

_____

_____

_____

_____

NOVEMBER 16

20___ _____
_____
_____
_____
_____

20___ _____
_____
_____
_____
_____

20___ _____
_____
_____
_____
_____

20___ _____
_____
_____
_____
_____

20___ _____
_____
_____
_____
_____

NOVEMBER 17

20___

20___

20___

20___

20___

NOVEMBER 18

20___ _____
_____
_____
_____
_____

20___ _____
_____
_____
_____
_____

20___ _____
_____
_____
_____
_____

20___ _____
_____
_____
_____
_____

20___ _____
_____
_____
_____
_____

NOVEMBER 19

20___ _____

_____

_____

_____

_____

20___ _____

_____

_____

_____

_____

20___ _____

_____

_____

_____

_____

20___ _____

_____

_____

_____

_____

20___ _____

_____

_____

_____

_____

NOVEMBER 20

20___ _____
_____
_____
_____
_____

20___ _____
_____
_____
_____
_____

20___ _____
_____
_____
_____
_____

20___ _____
_____
_____
_____
_____

20___ _____
_____
_____
_____

NOVEMBER 21

20___ _____
_____
_____
_____
_____

20___ _____
_____
_____
_____
_____

20___ _____
_____
_____
_____
_____

20___ _____
_____
_____
_____
_____

20___ _____
_____
_____
_____
_____

NOVEMBER 22

20___ _____

20___ _____

20___ _____

20___ _____

20___ _____

NOVEMBER 23

20___ _____

20___ _____

20___ _____

20___ _____

20___ _____

NOVEMBER 24

20___

_____

_____

_____

_____

20___

_____

_____

_____

_____

20___

_____

_____

_____

_____

20___

_____

_____

_____

_____

20___

_____

_____

_____

_____

NOVEMBER 25

20___

20___

20___

20___

20___

NOVEMBER 26

20_____ _____

_____

_____

_____

_____

20_____ _____

_____

_____

_____

_____

20_____ _____

_____

_____

_____

_____

20_____ _____

_____

_____

_____

_____

20_____ _____

_____

_____

_____

_____

NOVEMBER 27

20___ _____

20___ _____

20___ _____

20___ _____

20___ _____

NOVEMBER 28

20___ _____

_____

_____

_____

_____

20___ _____

_____

_____

_____

_____

20___ _____

_____

_____

_____

_____

20___ _____

_____

_____

_____

_____

20___ _____

_____

_____

_____

_____

NOVEMBER 29

20____ _____

20____ _____

20____ _____

20____ _____

20____ _____

NOVEMBER 30

20___ _____

_____

_____

_____

_____

20___ _____

_____

_____

_____

_____

20___ _____

_____

_____

_____

20___ _____

_____

_____

_____

20___ _____

_____

_____

_____

_____

DECEMBER 1

20____ _____
_____
_____
_____
_____

20____ _____
_____
_____
_____
_____

20____ _____
_____
_____
_____
_____

20____ _____
_____
_____
_____
_____

20____ _____
_____
_____
_____
_____

DECEMBER 2

20___ _____

20___ _____

20___ _____

20___ _____

20___ _____

DECEMBER 3

20___ _____

20___ _____

20___ _____

20___ _____

20___ _____

DECEMBER 4

20___ _____

_____

_____

_____

_____

20___ _____

_____

_____

_____

_____

20___ _____

_____

_____

_____

_____

20___ _____

_____

_____

_____

_____

20___ _____

_____

_____

_____

_____

DECEMBER 5

20___ _____
_____
_____
_____
_____

20___ _____
_____
_____
_____
_____

20___ _____
_____
_____
_____
_____

20___ _____
_____
_____
_____
_____

20___ _____
_____
_____
_____
_____

DECEMBER 6

20____ _____

_____

_____

_____

_____

20____ _____

_____

_____

_____

_____

20____ _____

_____

_____

_____

_____

20____ _____

_____

_____

_____

_____

20____ _____

_____

_____

_____

_____

DECEMBER 7

20___ _____
_____
_____
_____
_____

20___ _____
_____
_____
_____
_____

20___ _____
_____
_____
_____
_____

20___ _____
_____
_____
_____
_____

20___ _____
_____
_____
_____
_____

DECEMBER 8

20___

20___

20___

20___

20___

DECEMBER 9

20___ _____

20___ _____

20___ _____

20___ _____

20___ _____

DECEMBER 10

20___ _____
_____
_____
_____
_____

20___ _____
_____
_____
_____
_____

20___ _____
_____
_____
_____
_____

20___ _____
_____
_____
_____
_____

20___ _____
_____
_____
_____
_____

DECEMBER 11

20____ _____

_____

_____

_____

_____

20____ _____

_____

_____

_____

_____

20____ _____

_____

_____

_____

_____

20____ _____

_____

_____

_____

_____

20____ _____

_____

_____

_____

_____

DECEMBER 12

20___ _____

_____

_____

_____

_____

20___ _____

_____

_____

_____

_____

20___ _____

_____

_____

_____

_____

20___ _____

_____

_____

_____

_____

20___ _____

_____

_____

_____

_____

DECEMBER 13

20____ _____

_____

_____

_____

_____

20____ _____

_____

_____

_____

_____

20____ _____

_____

_____

_____

_____

20____ _____

_____

_____

_____

_____

20____ _____

_____

_____

_____

_____

DECEMBER 14

20___ _____

_____

_____

_____

_____

20___ _____

_____

_____

_____

_____

20___ _____

_____

_____

_____

_____

20___ _____

_____

_____

_____

_____

20___ _____

_____

_____

_____

_____

DECEMBER 15

20___

_____

_____

_____

_____

_____

20___

_____

_____

_____

_____

_____

20___

_____

_____

_____

_____

_____

20___

_____

_____

_____

_____

_____

20___

_____

_____

_____

_____

_____

DECEMBER 16

20___ _____

20___ _____

20___ _____

20___ _____

20___ _____

DECEMBER 17

20____ _____
_____
_____
_____
_____

20____ _____
_____
_____
_____
_____

20____ _____
_____
_____
_____
_____

20____ _____
_____
_____
_____
_____

20____ _____
_____
_____
_____
_____

DECEMBER 18

20___ _____
_____
_____
_____
_____

20___ _____
_____
_____
_____
_____

20___ _____
_____
_____
_____
_____

20___ _____
_____
_____
_____
_____

20___ _____
_____
_____
_____
_____

DECEMBER 19

20___ _____

_____

_____

_____

_____

20___ _____

_____

_____

_____

_____

20___ _____

_____

_____

_____

_____

20___ _____

_____

_____

_____

_____

20___ _____

_____

_____

_____

_____

DECEMBER 20

20___ _____

_____

_____

_____

_____

20___ _____

_____

_____

_____

_____

20___ _____

_____

_____

_____

_____

20___ _____

_____

_____

_____

_____

20___ _____

_____

_____

_____

_____

DECEMBER 21

20___ _____

20___ _____

20___ _____

20___ _____

20___ _____

DECEMBER 22

20___ _____

20___ _____

20___ _____

20___ _____

20___ _____

DECEMBER 23

20___ _____

_____

_____

_____

_____

20___ _____

_____

_____

_____

_____

20___ _____

_____

_____

_____

_____

20___ _____

_____

_____

_____

_____

20___ _____

_____

_____

_____

_____

DECEMBER 24

20___ _____

_____

_____

_____

_____

20___ _____

_____

_____

_____

_____

20___ _____

_____

_____

_____

_____

20___ _____

_____

_____

_____

_____

20___ _____

_____

_____

_____

_____

DECEMBER 25

20___ _____

20___ _____

20___ _____

20___ _____

20___ _____

DECEMBER 26

20___ _____

20___ _____

20___ _____

20___ _____

20___ _____

DECEMBER 27

20___ _____

_____

_____

_____

_____

20___ _____

_____

_____

_____

_____

20___ _____

_____

_____

_____

_____

20___ _____

_____

_____

_____

_____

20___ _____

_____

_____

_____

_____

DECEMBER 28

20 _____ _____

_____

_____

_____

_____

20 _____ _____

_____

_____

_____

_____

20 _____ _____

_____

_____

_____

_____

20 _____ _____

_____

_____

_____

_____

20 _____ _____

_____

_____

_____

_____

DECEMBER 29

20___ _____

20___ _____

20___ _____

20___ _____

20___ _____

DECEMBER 30

20___ _____

_____

_____

_____

_____

_____

20___ _____

_____

_____

_____

_____

_____

20___ _____

_____

_____

_____

_____

_____

20___ _____

_____

_____

_____

_____

_____

20___ _____

_____

_____

_____

_____

DECEMBER 31

20___ _____
_____
_____
_____
_____

20___ _____
_____
_____
_____
_____

20___ _____
_____
_____
_____
_____

20___ _____
_____
_____
_____
_____

20___ _____
_____
_____
_____
_____

DATES TO REMEMBER

DATES TO REMEMBER